To Dylan,
Love Mom & Dad
2015

The Very Special Baby

HARVEST HOUSE PUBLISHERS
EUGENE, OREGON

Mary Is Chosen by God

Mary lived in Galilee in a town called Nazareth. She was engaged to a carpenter named Joseph. One day, an angel appeared before her.

"Do not be afraid," he told the startled girl. "God has chosen you for a very special honor. You will give birth to a son, and you are to call him Jesus. He will be God's own Son, and his kingdom will never end!"

Mary was filled with wonder. "How can this be?" she asked softly. "I am not even married!"

"Everything is possible for God," replied the angel.

Mary bowed her head humbly, saying, "It will be as God wills it."

God Speaks to Joseph

When Joseph found out that Mary was going to have a baby, he thought she had been unfaithful to him and was very upset. He decided to break off the marriage, but before he could do anything, God spoke to him in a dream:

"Mary has not been unfaithful. The baby she is carrying was conceived from the Holy Spirit. She will give birth to a son, and you will call him Jesus, for he will save his people from their sins."

When Joseph awoke, he felt so much happier. Mary had been true to him, and now he would do all he could to keep her and the child safe. So they were married without delay!

Traveling to Bethlehem

Now, around this time, the emperor of Rome ordered a census of all the people he ruled over. He wanted to make sure that everyone paid their taxes! All the people throughout the lands ruled by Rome had to go to their hometown to be counted.

Joseph's family was descended from King David, and so he and Mary had to travel to Bethlehem, where King David had been born. Mary's baby was due to be born any day, and the journey was long and hard, but they had to do as the emperor ordered.

No Room at the Inn

When Mary and Joseph finally arrived in Bethlehem, they were tired and desperately wanted to find a room for the night, for the time had come for Mary's baby to be born.

But the town was filled to bursting, for everyone had come to be counted. Every single inn was full. There was nowhere for them to stay!

Born in a Manger

At last, an innkeeper said to them, "I have no rooms free, but there is somewhere you can spend the night," and he showed them to a stable where the animals were kept. It was dirty and smelly, but it was the best they could do.

That night, Mary's baby was born. She wrapped him in strips of cloth and then laid him gently on clean straw in a manger. Mary and Joseph looked down upon their son with joy, and they named him Jesus, just as the angel had told them to.

The Shepherds on the Hillside

That same night, some shepherds were keeping watch over their flocks in the hills above Bethlehem. Suddenly the sky was filled with a blinding light!

As they fell to the ground in fear, an angel spoke to them. "Do not be afraid. I bring you good news. Today in the town of David a Savior has been born to you; he is the Messiah, the Lord. Go and see for yourselves. You will find him wrapped in cloths and lying in a manger."

Then the whole sky was filled with angels praising God!

The Baby King

When the angels had left, the shepherds looked at one another in amazement. They could hardly believe what had just happened! But they all knew one thing— they simply had to go down to Bethlehem to see this baby with their own eyes!

The shepherds made sure that the sheep were safe and then hurried down to Bethlehem as fast as they could. They made their way to the stable, and there they found the baby lying in the manger just as they had been told. Filled with wonder and awe, the shepherds fell to their knees before the tiny baby boy who would change the world forever.

Then they rushed off to tell everyone the wonderful news!

Following a Star

In a distant land, three wise men had been studying the stars. When they found a really bright star shining in the skies, they followed it all the way to Judea, for they believed it was a sign that a great king had been born.

They asked King Herod in Jerusalem if he could show them the way to the baby who would be the king of the Jews. Herod was horrified! He didn't want another king around! His advisors told him of a prophecy that the new king would be born in the city of King David, in Bethlehem.

Then the cunning king sent the wise men to Bethlehem, saying, "Once you have found him, come back and tell me where he is, so that I can visit him too!"

Gifts for a King

The wise men followed the star to Bethlehem, where they found baby Jesus in a humble house.

There they knelt before him and presented him with fine gifts of gold, sweet-smelling frankincense, and a spicy ointment called myrrh.

Then they left to begin their long journey home–but they did not stop off at Herod's palace, for God had warned them in a dream not to tell Herod where the baby was!

Escape to Egypt

Herod was furious when he realized the wise men weren't coming back. Determined there should be no other king to challenge him, he gave an order that all boys under the age of two should be killed!

But no sooner had the wise men left Bethlehem than an angel appeared to Joseph in a dream, warning him to flee that very night to Egypt with Mary and Jesus, for Herod would be sending soldiers to search for the baby and to kill him.

Joseph and Mary swiftly gathered together their belongings and, lifting baby Jesus gently from his sleep, set off in haste on the long journey to Egypt.

Growing Up in Nazareth

Mary, Joseph and Jesus lived in Egypt until wicked King Herod died. After the death of Herod, they traveled back to Israel, but they did not return to Judea, for they learned that Herod's son was the new king, and if anything, he was worse than his father! Instead, they returned home to Nazareth.

As the years passed, Jesus grew to be filled with grace and wisdom. God loved him, and so did everyone who knew him.

The Very Special Baby

©2014 (North America) International Publishing
Services Pty Ltd. Sydney Australia.
www.ipsoz.com , External Markets © NPP Ltd Bath

Published by Harvest House Publishers
Eugene, Oregon 97402
www.harvesthousepublishers.com

ISBN 978-0-7369-6154-7

Printed in China

14 15 16 17 18 19 20 21 / IPS / 10 9 8 7 6 5 4 3 2 1